An Hachette UK Company
www.hachette.co.uk

Summersdale Publishers Ltd
Part of Octopus Publishing Group Limited
Carmelite House
50 Victoria Embankment
LONDON
EC4Y 0DZ
UK

www.summersdale.com

Printed and bound in China

ISBN: 978-1-80007-020-2

Substantial discounts on bulk quantities of Summersdale books are available to corporations, professional associations and other organizations. For details contact general enquiries: telephone: +44 (0) 1243 771107 or email: enquiries@summersdale.com.

DISCLAIMER: No animals were harmed or intoxicated in the making of this book.

I may have had
a few wines.

Slow down, Chester!
This is hard enough when
I've not had six pints!

**Come on then
if you think you're
hard enough.**

I AM OFF MY FURRY FACE
AND I AM LOVING IT.

SSSHSHSH…
PLEASE, MY
HEAD'S SPINNING!

Hooch ain't just for the pooch.

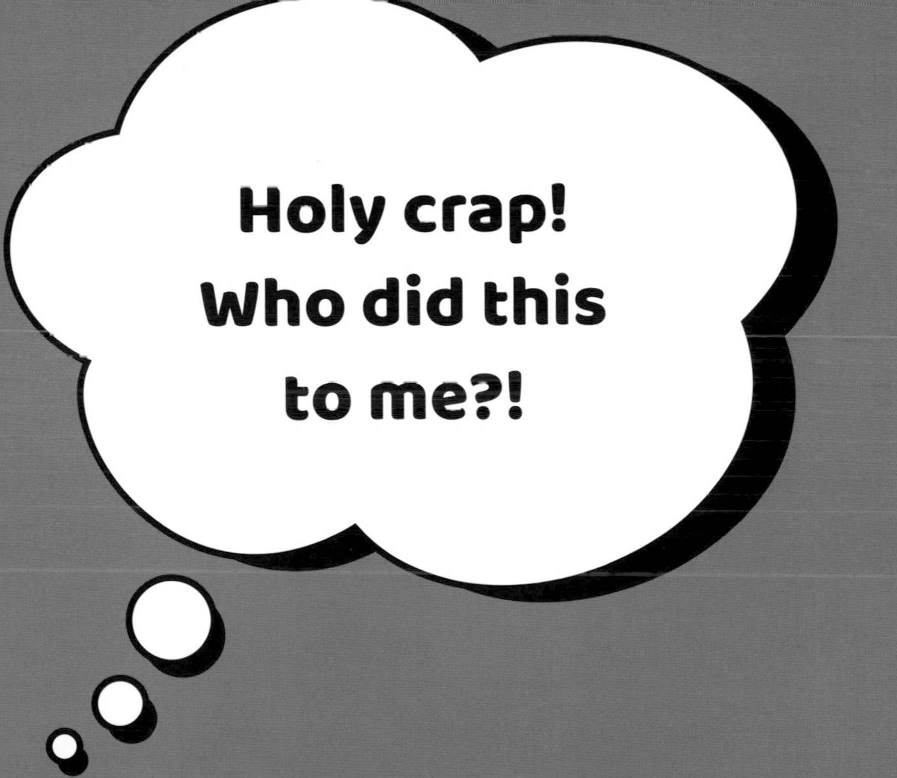
Holy crap!
Who did this
to me?!

HEY, HUMAN,
HOW DID YOU GET
UPSIDE-DOWN LIKE THAT?
AND WHY ARE YOU
STARTING TO SPIN?

Show me the way
to go home.

One gin,
two gins,
three gins,
floor.

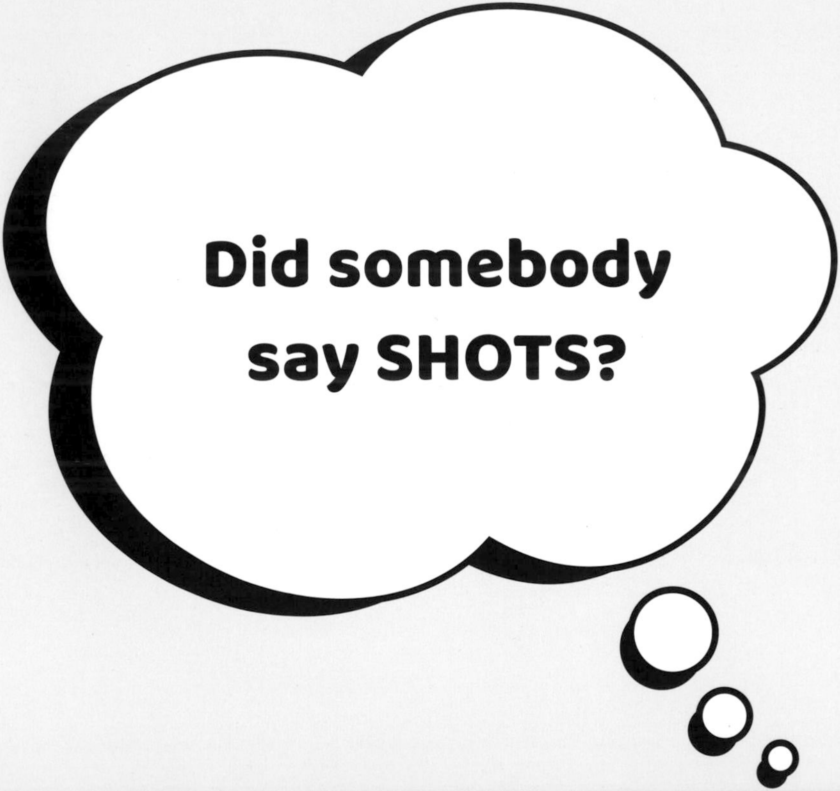
Did somebody
say SHOTS?

Why oh why did I stay out for "just one more"? And Sharon needs these reports by noon. Bleurgh.

Beer goggles
or not, that is
one fine feline.

I DON'T KNOW ANYTHING ABOUT HOW THAT MESS GOT THERE. I WAS TUCKED UP IN BED ALL NIGHT. HONEST.

CAN'T MOVE.
EVERYTHING ACHES.

Err, last night,
did we do what
I think we did?

WINE TIME!

THAT FEELING WHEN YOU REMEMBER WHAT YOU BLURTED OUT LAST NIGHT...

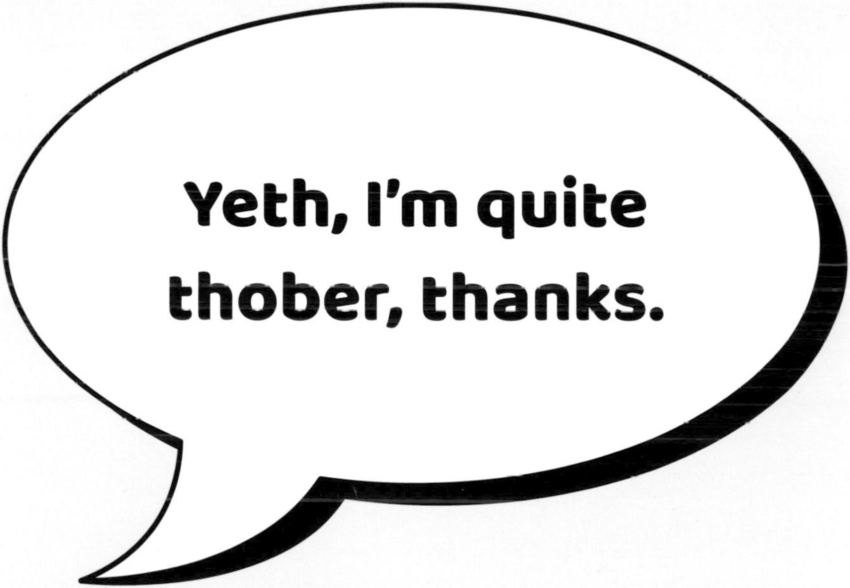
Yeth, I'm quite thober, thanks.

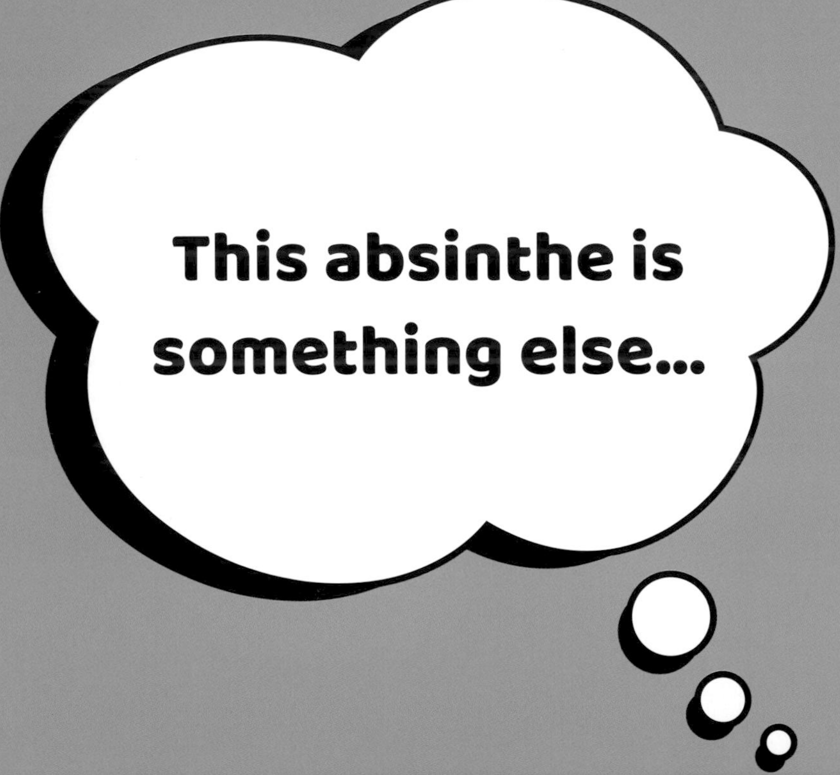
This absinthe is something else...

Walk of shame?
Nah, stride of pride!

**Any more
of that sweet,
sweet booze?**

Just gonna go lie
down in here in the
dark for 18 hours.

Stop impersonating me and going round to see my missus, you cad!

I HOPE THE HUMAN WON'T MIND ME USING THEIR FAVOURITE MUG TO UNLOAD ALL THIS BOOZY BARF.

I CAN TASTE IT
ON YOU, PERCY!

Don’t come in!
Just give me a minute.

No Dad, I hhh-haven't
been anyyywhere
nearrrr your whiskey.

I think I just sh*t myself.

MAYBE BUYING A
PLANE TICKET AT 3.00 A.M.
WAS NOT SUCH A GOOD IDEA,
COME TO THINK OF IT.

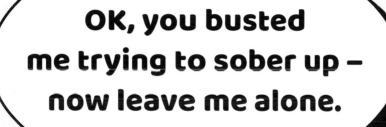

No, sir – I haven’t had a drop.

Not quite what I
had in mind when you
offered me something
icy cold to lap up!

Oh you want to judge *me*? Stick a cork in it.

I don't even know my own name right now, Megan, let alone who's the cutest kitty in the whole wide world.

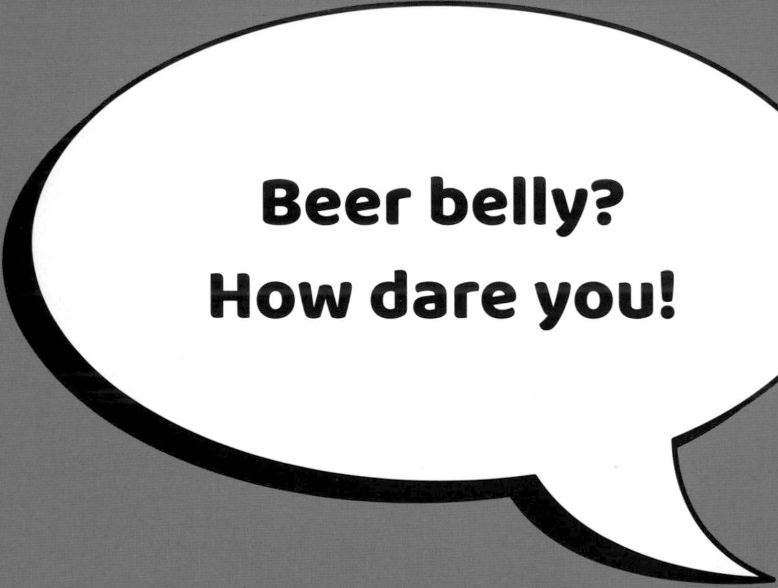
Beer belly?
How dare you!

PLAY IT COOL, LARRY.
I'M YOUR WINGCAT AND
YOU'RE MINE. THESE
LUCKY LADIES ARE ABOUT
TO HIT THE JACKPOT.

LUCKILY THE HUMAN IS DRIVING, SO I AM GETTING *WRECKED* ON THIS ROAD TRIP.

Bartender!
One more
refill, please!

Shall I knock this back,
or knock it off?
Decisions, decisions...

I am definitely not feline fine this morning.

YOU'RRREEE MY BEESSST FRIEND, YOU ARE!

Image credits

Have you enjoyed this book? If so, find us on Facebook at **Summersdale Publishers**, on Twitter at **@Summersdale** and on Instagram at **@summersdalebooks** and get in touch. We'd love to hear from you!

www.summersdale.com